All About
Breaking

Cameron Macintosh

All About Breaking

Text: Cameron Macintosh
Publishers: Tania Mazzeo and Eliza Webb
Series consultant: Amanda Sutera
  Hands on Heads Consulting
Editor: Gemma Smith
Project editor: Annabel Smith
Designer: Leigh Ashforth
Project designer: Danielle Maccarone
Illustrations: Mario Gushiken
Permissions researcher: Liz McShane
Production controller: Renee Tome

Acknowledgements
We would like to thank the following for permission to reproduce copyright material:

Front cover: Getty Images/Ryan Pierse; pp. 1, 7 (top right): Getty Images/PhotoStock-Israel; pp. 3, 7 (top left): Dreamstime.com/Dmytro Konstantynov; p. 4 (left): Shutterstock.com/chaossart, (right): iStock. com/chaoss; p. 5: iStock.com/warrengoldswain; p. 6 (top left): Shutterstock.com/Bohdan Malitskiy, (top right, p. 23): Shutterstock. com/Leika production, (bottom left, back cover bottom): Shutterstock. com/Master1305, (bottom right): Shutterstock.com/Vitalii Smulskyi; p. 7 (bottom left, back cover top): Dreamstime.com/Dmytro Konstantynov, (bottom right, p. 24): Shutterstock.com/Artur Didyk; p. 8: Getty Images/Linda Vartoogian; p. 9 (top): Getty Images/Andres Hernandez, (bottom): Getty Images/Mirrorpix; p. 10: Getty Images/Handout; p. 11 (top): AUSBreaking/Johnny Chaing, (bottom): AUSBreaking/Johnny Chaing; p. 12: Getty Images/Ryan Pierse; p. 13: Getty Images/Mark Kolbe; p. 14: Getty Images/Pier Marco Tacca; p. 15: Getty Images/LIONEL BONAVENTURE; p. 16: Getty Images/EITAN ABRAMOVICH; p. 17 (top): Reproduced with permission from International Olympic Committee (IOC), (bottom): Getty Images/Ryan Pierse; p. 18 (left): Dreamstime. com/Iakov Filimonov, (right): Shutterstock.com/DavidTB, pp. 4, 9, 11, 12, 18, background pattern: stock.adobe.com/Viktoria, pp. 19–22, background pattern: stock.adobe.com/Themeaseven.

Every effort has been made to trace and acknowledge copyright. However, if any infringement has occurred, the publishers tender their apologies and invite the copyright holders to contact them.

NovaStar

ISBN 978 0 17 033419 8

Cengage Learning Australia
Level 5, 80 Dorcas Street
Southbank VIC 3006 Australia
Phone: 1300 790 853
Email: aust.nelsonprimary@cengage.com

For learning solutions, visit **cengage.com.au**

Printed in China by 1010 Printing International Ltd
1 2 3 4 5 6 7 28 27 26 25 24

Nelson acknowledges the Traditional Owners and Custodians of the lands of all First Nations Peoples. We pay respect to Elders past and present, and extend that respect to all First Nations Peoples today.

Contents

What Is Breaking?	4
The History of Breaking	8
Breaking Today	10
Famous Breakers	12
Breaking at the Paris Olympics, 2024	16
Breaking For All	18
How to Toprock! (Procedure)	19
Glossary	23
Index	24

What Is **Breaking?**

Breaking, also known as breakdancing, is a high-energy, athletic style of dance. People who perform breaking are known as "breakers". Many of the moves performed by breakers are similar to movements from gymnastics and **martial arts**.

It takes a lot of strength and practice to perform breaking moves like these.

Breakers – also known as B-Girls and B-Boys – need to be strong and **flexible**. This helps them to perform many of the moves in breaking, like spinning on their backs or heads. These moves require a lot of skill and practice to be safe and to look **effortless**.

Although breaking began in the USA, it has become popular all around the world. Breaking is now a competitive sport as well as a dance style. Large breaking competitions are held in many countries.

In a head spin, a breaker balances on their head and spins their body.

There are four main types of move in breaking.

1 **Toprock**

Toprock is a combination of movements that breakers use at the beginning of a **set**. These moves are done standing up, before the breaker moves on to trickier moves on the floor.

2 **Downrock**

Downrock, also known as footwork, is made up of moves performed using the feet and hands lower down on the floor.

3 Freeze

A freeze is when a breaker comes to a standstill and holds a **pose**. The pose is usually held in an interesting position and takes exceptional strength and balance.

4 Power moves

Power moves are usually the most difficult moves breakers do. They often involve spinning and other **acrobatics**.

Breakers mostly make up their dances on the spot, combining moves that they have practised beforehand. Breaking is often competitive, with dancers "battling" each other to show who has the best moves.

The History of Breaking

People first began breaking in the USA in the 1970s. African American people, as well as Americans of **Caribbean** and **Latin** backgrounds, started breaking in the Bronx, a large area of New York City.

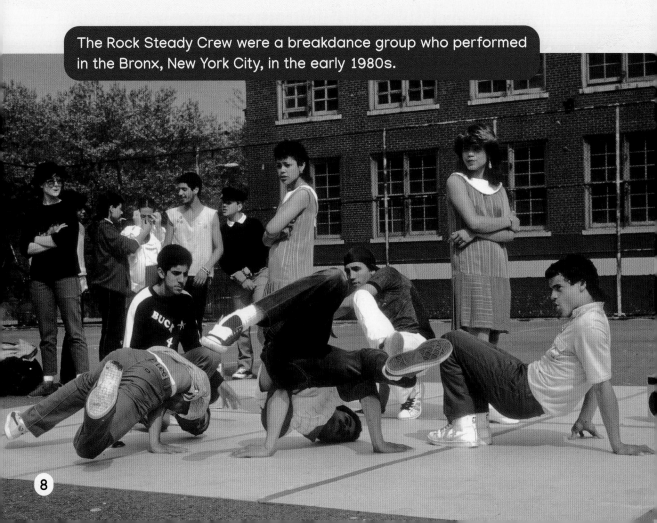

The Rock Steady Crew were a breakdance group who performed in the Bronx, New York City, in the early 1980s.

Breaking was, and still is, danced to the beats of **hip-hop** music. Breakers perform their moves to the "break" of a song – a short part of a song where just one instrument or beat is heard. In the early 1970s, a **DJ** named Kool Herc found a way to make the breaks longer. This allowed dancers to develop longer combinations of moves.

Breaking became even more popular in the 1980s, and featured in many movies and TV shows. In the 1990s the first international breaking competitions were held.

A crowd of people gather to watch a breaker perform on the street in the 1990s.

Breakdancers show their moves on a dance floor in England in 1998.

Breaking Today

Today, people of all ages and backgrounds enjoy breaking, both as dancers and spectators. Breaking is performed everywhere, including in public places like parks, town squares, car parks and footpaths.

Big breaking competitions are held all around the world. The World Dance Sport **Federation** holds the World Breaking Championships in a different country each year. Many countries also have tournaments of their own.

Breakdancers from the Netherlands and Korea compete in the Red Bull BC One world breakdancing competition in Paris, France, in 2023.

There is even a World Kids Breaking Championship. This is for dancers under the age of 18. Dancers can compete as individuals, in a **duo** or in groups.

To perform or compete, breakers usually gather in a circle, known as a **cypher**.

A young breakdancer performs in a street dance festival in Sydney in 2022.

Breakdancers gather in a cypher around a breaker at the Oceania Breaking Championships in Sydney in 2023.

Famous Breakers

Many breakers have become well-known around the world. Most of them have a stage name, which is what they call themselves when they perform. Here are some of the most successful breakers of recent years.

B-Girl Raygun

In 2023, Australia's top-ranked B-Girl was Rachael Gunn. Her stage name is B-Girl Raygun. Rachael won the 2023 Oceania Breaking Championships. She also researches and writes about breaking **culture**.

When Rachael started breaking in 2008, there were not many female breakers in Australia. Today, more and more girls and women have taken up breaking, inspired by dancers like Rachael.

B-Girl Raygun dances in Sydney in 2020.

B-Boy Akorn

Aron Mahuika, whose stage name is B-Boy Akorn, is one of Aotearoa New Zealand's most successful breakers. B-Boy Akorn is based in Christchurch, where he is a member of a **dance crew** called Common Ground.

B-Boy Akorn has competed around the world, winning many events including the Great Kiwi Break Off in 2023.

B–Boy Akorn performs in a B–Boy battle in Sydney in 2023.

B-Boy Victor

Victor Montalvo, whose stage name is B-Boy Victor, is a breaker based in Florida, USA. Victor's father was also a B-Boy in Mexico. Victor began breaking at the age of six, with guidance from his father. He first competed at the age of 11, and has won many competitions around the world, including the 2021 World Breaking Championship in Paris.

B–Boy Victor competes in the 2022 World Breaking Championship in South Korea.

B-Girl Sarah Bee

Sarah Bouyahyaoui (say: *Boo-yah-yoo-wee*), whose stage name is B-Girl Sarah Bee, was born in France. Sarah started breaking at the age of 11, and soon after joined a dance crew. Sarah is now part of an all-female dance crew called Zamounda, and has performed with well-known artists such as the famous singer Madonna.

Sarah has won many competitions, including the French Breaking Championship in 2022.

B-Girl Sarah Bee dances in Paris in 2019.

Breaking at the Paris Olympics, 2024

In 2020, it was announced that breaking would be included as an Olympic sport for the first time at the Paris Olympics in 2024. This decision was made after breaking was successfully introduced at the 2018 Youth Olympic Games in Buenos Aires, Argentina.

A breakdancer competes at the 2018 Youth Olympic Games.

The organisers of the 2024 Paris Olympics decided that breakers would compete against each other in one-on-one "battles" in front of a group of judges. Both men's and women's solo battles would be included over two days.

This is the official breaking logo of the 2024 Olympics.

Some of the best breakers from around the world compete at the 2024 Paris Olympics.

Breaking *For All*

Breaking is enjoyed by people of all abilities. It is a creative form of dance that encourages people to have fun and express themselves. It is also a great way to get fit, make new friends and learn more about hip-hop and its history.

People of all ages and abilities can try out breaking!

How to Toprock!

Toprock is one of the most important parts of breaking. It is the first thing breakers do in a performance as they enter the stage or cypher.

There are many forms of toprock. Here is one that is easy to learn. It is known as a crossover step.

Goal

To perform a toprock crossover step

Step

Stand straight, with your arms crossed over your chest.

Step ②

* Step your right leg forward across your body, and lean forward. As you do this, uncross your arms.

* Swing your left arm forward and your right arm back behind you. Your hips and shoulders should face in opposite directions, crossing over each other as you make this move.

Step ③

Return to the same position as in Step 1.

Step 4

* Step your left leg forward, across your body. As you do this, uncross your arms again.

* Swing your right arm forward and your left arm back behind you. Again, your hips and shoulders should cross over each other as you make this move.

Step 5

Return to the same position as in Step 1, and then repeat the other steps.

Step 6

Practise until you can perform your toprock smoothly, and repeat it several times over without stopping.

Glossary

acrobatics (*noun*) — movements with high levels of skill, strength or balance

Caribbean (*noun*) — from the Caribbean islands, which are located near Central America

culture (*noun*) — the ideas, customs and way of life of a group

cypher (*noun*) — a circle of people with one breaker dancing in the middle

dance crew (*noun*) — a group of dancers who dance together and help each other improve their dancing skills

DJ (*noun*) — short for disc jockey; a person who plays recorded music on the radio or at an event

duo (*noun*) — two people who perform together

effortless (*adjective*) — needing little or no effort, so that it seems easy

federation (*noun*) — a group of organisations that have come together

flexible (*adjective*) — able to easily move in a range of ways

hip-hop (*noun*) — a type of music with a strong beat, which often includes rap vocals

Latin (*noun*) — from Latin America, which includes Central and South America

martial arts (*noun*) — sports or skills that have been developed for combat or self-defence

pose (*noun*) — a particular way of standing or sitting

set (*noun*) — a series of actions or movements

Index

B–Boy Akorn   13

B–Boy Victor   14

B–Girl Raygun   12

B–Girl Sarah Bee   15

breaking competitions   5, 9,
    10–11, 12–15

championships   10, 11, 12, 14,
    15, 16–17

crossover step   19–22

cypher   11, 19, 23

DJ Kool Herc   9

downrock   6

freeze   7

gymnastics   4

hip-hop   9, 18, 23

martial arts   4, 23

New York City   8

Paris Olympics, 2024   16–17

power moves   5, 7

toprock   6, 19–22

World Dance Sport Federation   10

Youth Olympic Games   16